Saint Faustina Kowalska

Saint Faustina Kowalska

Messenger of Mercy

Written by
Susan Helen Wallace, FSP

Illustrated by
Joan Waites

Pauline
BOOKS & MEDIA
Boston

Library of Congress Cataloging-in-Publication Data

Wallace, Susan Helen, 1940–
 Saint Faustina Kowalska : messenger of mercy / written by Susan Helen Wallace ; illustrated by Joan Waites.
    p. cm. — (Encounter the saints series)
 ISBN 0-8198-7101-X (pbk.)
 1. Faustina, Saint, 1905–1938—Juvenile literature. 2. Christian saints—Poland—Biography—Juvenile literature. I. Waites, Joan C. II. Title.
 BX4700.F175W35 2007
 282.092—dc22
 [B]

                          2007001089

Saint Faustina's prayers are quoted from: *Diary of St. Maria Faustina Kowalska: Divine Mercy in My Soul* © 1987 Congregation of Marians of the Immaculate Conception, Stockbridge, MA 01263. www.marian.org. Used with permission.

The author gratefully acknowledges the kind assistance of the Sisters of Our Lady of Mercy in verifying details of Saint Faustina's life and spirituality.

"P" and PAULINE are registered trademarks of the Daughters of St. Paul.

Copyright © 2007, Daughters of St. Paul

Published by Pauline Books & Media, 50 Saint Paul's Avenue, Boston, MA 02130-3491. www.pauline.org.

Printed in the U.S.A.

SFMOM VSAUSAPEOILL4-2410150 7101-X

Pauline Books & Media is the publishing house of the Daughters of St. Paul, an international congregation of women religious serving the Church with the communications media.

5 6 7 8 9 10 11   23 22 21 20 19

Saint Ignatius of Loyola
For the Greater Glory of God

Saint Joan of Arc
God's Soldier

Saint John Paul II
Be Not Afraid

Saint Kateri Tekakwitha
Courageous Faith

Saint Martin de Porres
Humble Healer

Saint Maximilian Kolbe
Mary's Knight

Saint Pio of Pietrelcina
Rich in Love

Saint Teresa of Avila
Joyful in the Lord

Saint Thérèse of Lisieux
The Way of Love

Saint Thomas Aquinas
Missionary of Truth

Saint Thomas More
Courage, Conscience, and the King

*For even more titles in the
Encounter the Saints series,
visit: www.pauline.org.*

CONTENTS

1
A GIRL NAMED HELENA

"Helena, wait for Papa," Stanislaus Kowalski called. "Wait, I don't want you to fall!" The young farmer hurried along the crooked path lined with weeds and clusters of rocks. "Stay with me," he said, gently taking hold of four-year-old Helena's hand.

Helena's two older sisters, Josephine and Genevieve, were near the front door of the family cottage. Now that their chores were finished, they could play. Their mother, Marianna Kowalska, kept an eye on the girls as she went about her housework. (In Poland, many family names end in "-ski." Polish grammar provides both a masculine and a feminine ending for these names. This is why the men of Helena's family would spell their names with the ending "-ski"; the women, instead, would use the feminine ending of "-ska.")

Helena was different from her sisters, though. Although she was still too young to be of much help, she insisted on staying with Papa as he led the cows back to the barn every evening for milking. This little trip was a highlight of the child's day!

For the first nine years of their marriage, Stanislaus and Marianna had waited and prayed to have a family. Finally, their prayers had been answered. The couple would eventually have eight children, six girls and two boys. They were Josephine, Genevieve, Helena, Natalia, Stanislaus, Mecislaus, Marianna Lucyna, and Wanda. Two other children died as infants.

Their third child, Helena, had been born on August 25, 1905, in Glogowiec (pronounced Glog-o-wick), Poland. One day, she would become famous in her own country—and around the world—as Saint Faustina. But that would be many years from now.

Baby Helena was baptized at Saint Casimir Church soon after birth. From a very young age, the little girl loved to hear about Jesus, Mary, and the saints. Every evening she listened, entranced, as her father read wonderful true stories from his mission magazines.

"Will you read us stories of the saints tonight, Papa?" she asked each night.

"Of course, Helenka," Papa always responded with enthusiasm. ("Helenka" means "little Helen.") The children didn't know that every joint in his body was aching for some rest. Stanislaus often sighed and thought how wonderful it would be to rest for a little while. "But I can't disappoint the children," he told himself. Helena stood by the cabinet and watched Papa search for just the right magazine. She couldn't wait to learn how to read.

Helena quickly learned the short prayers her parents taught her, and she loved saying them over and over. Sometimes she simply murmured to herself, "Jesus, Mary, heaven." How beautiful those simple words were!

Once, when she was six, Helena woke up in the middle of the night. Sitting straight up in bed, she prayed in her clear voice: "My Jesus, I love you. Mother Mary, I love you. Take me to heaven with you some day." Helena's mother appeared in the doorway and gently encouraged her to lie down again. "It's time for all children to be sound asleep, Helena. You can say more prayers in the morning, as many prayers as you like." But the little girl wasn't convinced.

"Oh, no, Mama," she answered, shaking her head, "what if my guardian angel is waking me to pray? I just couldn't disappoint my angel!" Mama was amazed. Papa wrinkled his forehead, the way he did when he was a bit perplexed.

Stanislaus and Marianna were devoted parents and tried their best to practice their Catholic faith every day. They helped the children to understand that Sunday and feast day Masses were special events.

During the week, Stanislaus had to concentrate on coaxing the poor soil of his farm into growing wheat, rye, and crops for his cattle to graze on. He had a large—and growing—family to feed. Stanislaus was proud of their little cottage, made of stone and brick with wooden shingles on the roof. The cottage had three small rooms and a hallway. It was home.

Mama spent her busy days cooking, cleaning, and caring for her large family. Papa worked the farm in the early mornings and during late evenings. During the day, he labored at carpentry to earn enough money to feed and clothe them all. The couple's Catholic faith was as natural a part of their lives as running the farm.

They began each morning with prayers that set the tone for the day. Sometimes, when the sun was shining and the air was warm, Stanislaus sang hymns as he worked. God was always close by. Then, of course, there was Helena, who often tugged at his sleeve and asked him to pray with her. Each evening, the setting sun lit the hues of red in Helena's hair as father and daughter led the cows to the barn.

"Oh, Papa," Helena said one day, "I'm so excited about preparing for my first Confession and first Communion. I want to receive the sacraments, just like you and Mama. After all, I'm old enough now. I'm nine!"

Stanislaus smiled. "I'm happy for you, Helenka, really happy." Helena was always excited about something. It was a good reminder to Papa to recognize and cherish the many joyful moments in life.

Their parish priest, Father Pawlowski, had carefully prepared Helena and her companions for their first Holy Communion. "There's one more thing I would like to share with you," Father said solemnly. "This is an old Polish custom." The children listened intently. "I would like to invite you to make a special act of love for Jesus."

"How can we do that, Father?" the children asked.

"Before you leave the house to come to church for your first Communion Mass, go to your parents and kiss their hands. Then ask forgiveness for whatever you may have done wrong. This pleases Jesus very much," Father concluded.

"Yes, Father," the children chorused.

When Helena's first Communion day arrived, she kissed each of her parents' hands. "Papa, Mama, I'm so sorry for whatever I have done wrong. Please forgive me." Her parents took turns hugging her, and Helena felt really ready to go to church and receive Jesus in Holy Communion.

Helena continued to receive the sacrament of Penance every Saturday. She also wanted to make sure never to miss Mass on Sunday. What could she do to help her parents with the farm chores so that the whole family would be free to go to Mass? She realized that their three cows had to be milked even on Sunday. That took time. So the young girl invented an elaborate plan.

That Saturday night, Helena unlatched the bedroom window. Early the next morning, she crawled out the window and headed to the barn all by herself. The girl carefully led the cows to pasture.

A little while later, Papa got up and went to the barn to take his cows out to the field. The poor man shook the morning sleep from his eyes and stared, panicked. "Where are my cows? Stolen? I hope not!"

Mr. Kowalski ran out of the barn and stopped. There on the path was Helena, peacefully leading the three cows tied together by a single rope. All of Papa's fear and anger melted into a broad smile. "Now can we all go to Mass?" the girl asked eagerly.

"Yes, Helenka," Papa smiled, "thanks to you."

2

TELL US A STORY

Now that the Kowalski children were older, they took turns leading the cattle to pasture. On days when Helena came down the path with the cows, younger neighbors often showed up to join her. They were all different ages and full of fun.

"Helena, can we come with you?"

"Sure," the girl answered kindly. "Once the cows are safely in the field, we can sit down and have a story if you like."

"Yes!" came a happy chorus. The children sat in a circle, waiting. Helena loved an audience. Even more, she enjoyed making the children happy and teaching them about the saints.

"What will today's story be?" someone asked.

"It will be about Saint Francis of Assisi," Helena began, looking at each child. "Saint Francis was wonderful. He lived in Italy, the country where the pope lives. Saint Francis wanted to live the way Jesus lived his life."

"What does that mean?" asked a small boy.

"Well, Jesus lived a poor man's life. He was loving and obedient to his mother, Mary, and to Saint Joseph. He did good things whenever possible to make people's lives happier on this earth.

"Saint Francis studied the life of Jesus written in the Gospels. He wanted so much to be like Jesus that he gave away his fancy clothes, everything he owned—even his money."

"I don't know if I'd do that," murmured someone.

Helena continued, "Francis prayed often and went to Mass every day. He helped everyone in need. He was also kind and respectful to people, whether they were rich or poor. He wore a plain grayish robe tied with a cord at the waist.

"Other young men joined him. They made vows, sacred promises to their bishop, to be poor, pure, and obedient, trying to be like Jesus. This group grew and grew. They do so much good helping people to love Jesus. They're called Franciscans, after Saint Francis. Isn't that wonderful? Imagine all the good that just one saint can do."

The effects of World War I began to be felt throughout Poland. Children could still laugh and play, taking pleasure in simple things. Adults, though, were worried and fearful for the safety of their families. Word spread about famine and destruction in other parts of Poland.

Would the Kowalski family and their neighbors be spared? Papa worked hard to support the children, but the war made life for his family and for the general population even more difficult. Food was increasingly scarce. What a person didn't grow himself on his farm, he didn't have and couldn't get. Transportation and communication were at a standstill throughout the country. It seemed as if the Kowalski family's little village was frozen in time.

How could such poor people become poorer still? Here's one example. The Kowalska girls owned only one dress that was good enough to wear to Sunday Mass. They would never wear their faded, shabby work clothes to worship God. Because the girls were close enough in size, they took turns wearing their only dress, handmade by Mama, to Sunday Mass.

On the Sundays when it wasn't Helena's turn to go to Mass, she prayed alone in her favorite quiet corner at home. She prayed for as long as she thought the Mass was going on at her parish church. Sometimes Mama would call Helena to perform a chore. If Helena didn't respond right away, Mama realized the Mass must still be going on. As soon as prayer time was over, Helena would hurry to her mother and kiss her hand. "Don't be angry, Mama," she would say. "I was praying just as if I were there at church for Mass."

Even though the war continued, schools were reopened in 1917. Helena was twelve years old. She was enrolled in second grade in the nearby village of Swinice (pronounced Swy-ne-ce). Helena was very excited because she already knew how to read and was anxious to learn more. She was able to attend three semesters of school, until the spring of 1919. Reluctantly, the principal and staff had to tell Helena and the other disappointed students of her age that they would not be able to continue. A whole new group of eager children was waiting to come to school.

Papa had a lot on his mind that day as he went from chore to chore around the farm.

Life wasn't easy, he realized, but he and his family still had many blessings: *Lord, thank you for all your goodness to us. Please lighten the burden of my fellow Poles who suffer and live in fear.*

That was the right prayer for the times. Mr. Kowalski and a few of his neighbors were getting news from strangers wandering through their area. Invading troops had marched from Warsaw to Pinsk, now called Kraków (pronounced Krak-off), bringing death, destruction, and rapid starvation. They said that the 230-mile stretch of road was littered with the bodies of people unable to survive the hunger and cold.

During the winters of the war years, 1914–1918, the Kowalskis were often cold and hungry, too. Fortunately, no soldiers had come to their home to terrify and mistreat them. As for being poor, they could always make do. The children believed that Mama and Papa were there to solve any problems. Every day included a healthy dose of fun and laughter.

Mr. Kowalski breathed a sigh of relief and a prayer when some wonderful news finally came. On November 11, 1918, the war, which would be known to history as the Great War, and eventually as World War

I, was over. Stanislaus hugged his wife and children. This was reason to celebrate! Mama lit a candle in front of the picture of the Blessed Mother. Everyone knelt down and prayed a decade of the Rosary together. Then, Papa asked Mama to cook a special meal, the way only she could. Mama smiled. Would the day ever come when she would have a pantry full of ingredients to choose from? *Probably not,* she laughed to herself. *But other things are more important!*

3

A Secret of the Heart

Days, weeks, and months passed quickly into years. Helena had no opportunity for more schooling, but she knew how to keep busy on the farm. She was always on hand for her mother and father.

"Let me help," she'd say to Mama. "I'll clean up the kitchen." "I'll take care of the laundry." There was always something that needed to be done. Farm chores with Papa were important, too. Helena could milk the cows herself now, and Papa would carry the heavy pails into the kitchen. Daily routine was pretty ordinary again after the hard times Poland had been through. Life was peaceful in the Kowalski household. The only excitement came from the voices of children playing games outside in good weather.

When winter came, the winds howled and snow pelted the sturdy stone cottage. Mama, Papa, and the children were snug inside, gathered in the kitchen near the blazing fire. The children loved books, especially Papa's mission magazines. Helena read the exciting stories aloud now, so Papa could have a little time to relax. The children were growing up and getting better at doing chores, but nobody could cook like Mama. They could help her peel vegetables, though, and clean up. Of course, they all learned to wash the dishes, dry them, and put them away.

While Helena busied herself with useful tasks, her imagination was at work on a subject of its own. *I want to live for Jesus, to belong only to Jesus,* the girl thought. *I want so much to become a religious sister. I can't explain it because I've never even seen one. If only there was a convent in Glogowiec. I could visit and pray with the sisters and ask them so many questions.*

Meanwhile, she thought, *I can pray right here. I want to talk to you, Jesus. I want to listen to you and grow close to you. I want you to make your home in my heart.* Helena prayed quietly as she performed her chores. She prayed longer in the evening before bedtime.

Her parents discussed this situation together. They decided it would be best not to encourage her in the excessive prayerfulness that seemed to be overtaking her.

Instead, Papa urged her to keep excelling in household and farm tasks. Mama made a point of complimenting her on how responsible she was and how much she depended on Helena's hard work.

Helena loved Mama and Papa more than anybody in this world. She would never want to hurt them. She began to understand, though, that if she was called to religious life, she wouldn't lose her parents. She would love them even more because of her love for Jesus.

Sometimes, when she prayed, she seemed to see bright, beautiful lights. One day when this happened, she shared the joy of the experience with her parents. Helena noticed that Mama and Papa became uncomfortable. They glanced quickly at each other and remained quiet.

"Helena," Mama said at last, "Papa and I are having trouble believing you. It doesn't seem possible.... I mean about the lights. It would be better not to talk about them, all right?"

Helena nodded her head. "Of course, Mama," she said. The girl did stop talking about the beautiful lights, but she continued to see them just the same.

Helena was now sixteen years old. Mama gave her permission to work as a house-maid. Many teenage girls and young women in Poland did this to support themselves and to meet new people outside their home-towns. Meanwhile, Helena hoped; maybe something would happen to help her follow the vocation she really wanted. She prayed for the day when she would win her parents' consent. Until that day came, she would work.

Mrs. Bryszewska (pronounced Briz-zoo-ska) and her husband lived in Alexandrow, near Lodz, and owned a bakery. Helena, the new maid, would take care of their young son as well as help around the house. She moved in with her satchel of clothes and a few of Papa's mission magazines. She had never been away from her family before, and she missed them very much. But the Bryszewskis' little boy became her friend right away. He adored Helena and loved to hear her stories.

Helena continued to pray silently as she worked each day, and she often saw the strange bright lights as she prayed at night. One day, though, as she walked out of the Bryszewskis' house to the backyard, she gasped and began to shriek. "Fire! Fire in

*"Is there anything we can do
to change your mind?"*

the bakery!" she cried. Mrs. Bryszewska ran into the yard and caught her young maid as she collapsed. What was Helena screaming about? There was no fire!

Later that day, Helena admitted to her sister Josephine, who was visiting, that what she'd thought was a fire had really been the bright lights once again.

A year after Helena had come to stay with the family, she finally understood the meaning of the lights: they were blazing to lead her to God. The next day, she told Mrs. Bryszewska that she would be leaving.

"But why must you go?" the woman cried.

"I can't explain it," Helena said softly.

"Is there anything we can do to change your mind?" Mrs. Bryszewska asked. She could see the disappointment on her little son's face. For him, losing Helena would be like losing a big sister. Helena shook her head. How could she explain that she was more and more anxious to become closer to God? She was convinced that the best way for her to do this would be to enter religious life. Maybe now would be a good time to talk to Mama and Papa again about her vocation.

4

JESUS WAS WAITING

It was so good to be home! Helena hugged her parents, sisters, and brothers.

She rolled up her sleeves and put on an apron to help with the farm and kitchen work. There was always plenty to do!

Mama and Papa were surprised that Helena had left her job. What could have happened? Helena's mind was hard at work. It would just take a little time before she could bring up the subject. Her parents talked it over and wondered if, once again, Helena was having thoughts about a religious vocation.

They were right.

"Mama," Helena said with a smile, "I still want very much to follow Jesus and become a religious sister. It would mean more to me than anything else if you would just let me follow my vocation. I want you to be happy about it, too."

Mama shook her head. No! There was so much she wanted to explain, but the words wouldn't come out.

"Maybe Papa will let me talk to him about it," the girl said, trying to feel hopeful. Helena went outside and found him in the barn.

"Papa, I really have to talk with you," Helena said, trying to sound courageous. She thought she heard a little groan escape her father's lips. "Papa," the girl said, "I still want to be a sister."

"I thought so," Papa said gently. "I have a problem with it, because joining a religious order will require that you have a dowry." He took her hand. "You know we don't have the money, Helenka. Mama and I are just barely able to keep the farm going. The economy is bad in Poland right now. Girls who enter convents usually bring some kind of a dowry to help the congregation financially. We can't offer anything for you to bring."

"Papa, I don't need any money," the girl said. "Jesus himself will lead me to the convent." Mr. Kowalski shook his head. He admired Helena's faith and youthful courage.

She's such a good girl, he thought, as tears came to his eyes. *But*, he asked himself, *will faith take care of her and protect her from all the dangers facing our country? Will faith put bread on her table and a roof over her head? She's just a child.*

"I can't say yes, Helena. You'd be too far from home. If something happened, we wouldn't be able to protect you. If you needed something, we wouldn't know. We'd rather have you stay at home. Or at least," he said as an afterthought, "get another job in Lodz. That's nearby. You'll get more experience and be a little independent, too. You can be close enough that Mama and I won't have to worry so much."

Helena got her job in Lodz. She worked for three unmarried ladies. She liked them right away and they liked her. The women went to Mass daily and allowed Helena to go as well. She was also permitted to make brief visits to any ill or housebound neighbors who needed a kind word and someone to pray with them. Helena brought them comfort. Neighbors who were dying would find courage for their journey to paradise. Helena's new employers went regularly to receive the sacrament of Reconciliation. The parish priest, who was their confessor, became her confessor, too.

Helena worked for the ladies but lived with a relative, Michael Rapacki, and his family. This pleased her parents, who were always concerned about her safety and welfare.

"Do you still want to be a sister?" Uncle Michael would tease. Helena didn't let him embarrass her.

"I will become a sister," the teenager told him firmly. "That's what I've wanted since I was a little girl."

Uncle Michael wasn't put off by Helena's no-nonsense replies. He brought it up again and again. Soon Helena began to look for other work, but a voice inside her still urged, "Leave the world and join a convent."

She decided to return home for a while, at least until she could figure out what to do. Her life was going nowhere. She was seventeen now, and Jesus seemed to be pulling her toward a life spent totally for him. How would she get there? She wasn't allowed to follow her longings. *What's the use?* the young woman concluded, *God wants one thing, but my parents want another.*

A brief new chapter of Helena's life began. She blocked out the desires of the Spirit in her soul and chose to fill her life with what the world could offer her. She bought some attractive clothes and had her hair styled. She and her sisters went to dances and spent happy times with other young people their age. "What else can I do?" she asked herself. Somehow, though, she was never at peace.

Helena applied for her next job through an employment agency. The agency sent her to be interviewed by a mother with three young children. Mrs. Marcianna Sadowska welcomed Helena, but couldn't help noticing the young woman's fancy clothes and attractive appearance. *Caring for three little children might not be to her liking,* the young mother said to herself. *This probably won't work.* Her doubts were reflected in her face.

Helena understood what the woman was thinking. "Mrs. Sadowska, I really need the job, and I know I'll enjoy the children. I'll take good care of them. Please, give me a chance!"

The woman looked at her searchingly, and then smiled at Helena's earnest expression. "I'll give you the job," she said, "and we'll see how things go."

Helena reported for work on February 2, 1923. The three little children couldn't have been happier with Helena. She loved them, too. Mrs. Sadowska was very relieved. She could help her husband in their grocery store without worrying.

One day, Helena had a pleasant surprise. Her oldest sister, Josephine, came to visit. Mrs. Sadowska was very happy for her.

"Helena, run down to the store and get some nice treats for you and your sister. Whatever you'd like!"

Helena darted down the stairs and was back quickly. She held one sticky bun, wrapped in white paper, in her hand.

"Is that all you got?" her employer asked.

"Oh, this is plenty," Helena assured her. The girls divided the pastry between them and chatted happily. After Helena had learned how all the family was and how the farm was going, Josephine carefully brought up the main purpose of her visit.

"You know, Helena, Mama and Papa want you to come home. They miss you and worry about whether you're safe and well. We all miss you. It's not the same without our Helena. And the neighbors' children still come by, asking for you."

Helena smiled and said in her heart what she couldn't say to her sister: *I still want to become a religious sister. I want to live for Jesus.*

Instead, she said simply, "Josephine, I won't be coming with you." Her sister was disappointed, but she understood.

Too restless to stay any longer, and still longing to find a way to follow her vocation, Helena left the Sadowski family on July 1, 1924. She had worked there for a year and five months.

5

DRIFTING

Helena was still drifting, still frustrated, still trying to find her way to religious life. She was convinced of her choice, but how would she make it happen? She would be nineteen in August.

One evening, she and one of her sisters were in Lodz with Uncle Michael's family. They decided to go to a dance. Helena wore a beautiful dress and looked very happy as she danced with other young people. She appreciated the attention and was enjoying herself.

Suddenly, she was overtaken by an intensely sad feeling. It wasn't caused by anything that was happening at the dance. What was going on?

As she danced, she felt a presence beside her. She saw a person at her side. It was Jesus! There was no doubt in her mind—it was Jesus, the wounded, bleeding, suffering Christ.

The girl gazed into the Master's eyes. He sadly asked her, "How long will it take?

How long will you keep putting me off?" A moment later, the vision ended.

Oh, a shaken Helena asked herself, *how long? I need courage and strength from you, Jesus.* She slipped away from the dance. All alone, she made her way to the nearby Cathedral of Saint Stanislaus Kostka. There Helena prayed and asked for guidance. What should be her next step?

Dear Jesus, what do you want me to do? In her soul, the young woman heard the Lord's reply: "Go at once to Warsaw; there you will find a convent to enter."

Uncle Michael took her to the train station. "This is serious," Uncle Michael said, trying to remain calm. "Your parents will be worried and disappointed." He wasn't teasing now. He was worried, too. He would have to explain it all to Helena's parents. That wouldn't be easy. The young woman looked straight ahead as she handed her ticket to the conductor and boarded the train to Warsaw. There was no turning back.

As she sat alone, looking out the window, tears slid quietly down Helena's cheeks. She had only the clothes she was wearing. She had left her elegant wardrobe behind. *Jesus will take care of me,* she told herself. Helena felt she was doing what Jesus wanted. That was what she wanted, too.

As the train slowed down and glided into the Warsaw station, Helena waited her turn to get off. She looked around. What a big city! It wasn't at all like her little village of dirt roads and small farms. Suddenly, the girl was frightened.

I don't know anybody here, she said to herself, *not one person. Mary, Mother of God, please guide me.* Faustina heard the reply in her heart: "Leave the city and go to the village nearby." She obeyed, and in that village she found lodging for the night.

The next morning, Faustina returned to the city. She walked a short distance and soon came upon Saint James Catholic Church. The young woman pulled open the heavy door and went in. A priest was celebrating Mass. Helena heard the voice in her soul: "Go to that priest and tell him everything. He will tell you what to do next."

When Mass was finished, Helena went to the sacristy and knocked respectfully on the partially opened door. Father James Dabrowski invited his guest to sit down as altar servers busied themselves putting away the vestments and vessels that had just been used for the Mass. The priest listened as Helena explained why she was there.

"Oh, Father, please help me." Cautiously, Helena told him her story. She explained her longing for religious life, her parents' opposition, and her vision of Jesus at the dance in Lodz. The priest listened intently.

"How is it that you are here this morning?" Father asked.

"During Mass, a voice in my heart said very clearly, 'Go to that priest and tell him everything. He will tell you what to do next,'" said Helena simply.

Something in Father Dabrowski's own heart softened as the young woman, a total stranger, told her story. He decided that he would help her.

"Helena, why don't we start this way?" He took out a small pad of paper and a pen and wrote a name and address.

"This is a fine family I know. They live in this parish and are looking for a maid. During your free time, you can visit nearby convents. Live with the family until you find the convent you want to enter."

Helena went directly to her new employer, Mrs. Lipszyc, and presented the note from the pastor. It was simple and direct, explaining that the young woman, a stranger to the city, needed employment. The rest of the story would unfold in God's time, Father Dabrowski wrote. Mrs. Lipszyc took Helena in.

Helena was healthy-looking and cheerful, neat and clean. Despite that, she knocked on many convent doors before finding a sister who would permit her to even step inside for a visit. Many of the people in Warsaw were poor and struggling. The war had left devastation. Some convents may have worried that young women who were not truly called to religious life might seek admission just to have a place to live and food to eat. But Helena was sincerely following a call to religious life. She simply wouldn't give up.

One afternoon, Helena appeared on the doorstep of the Sisters of Our Lady of Mercy at 3/9 Zytnia Street. She had never met any of these sisters or even heard of the congregation. The building looked old and drab. Helena watched the heavy front door slowly creak open. A voice asked kindly, "What do you want, young lady?"

"I want to become a sister," Helena said hopefully.

The sister invited her in and went to get Mother Superior. Helena waited, her heart thumping.

Soon Mother Michael entered the room. She was kind and serene. Helena felt at home with her. At least these sisters were willing to talk to her and listen to what she had to say!

Mother Michael had intended to ask Helena a few general questions and then graciously send her away. The more they talked, though, the more the sister was impressed by this young stranger. She seemed practical, intelligent, and honest. She was hardworking, too. Her hands, reddened and chafed from cooking and cleaning, revealed that.

"Mother," said Helena timidly, "I know that sisters generally bring a dowry to help the congregation. I am poor, and I have no dowry. Yet I feel in my heart that Jesus is calling me to religious life. What can I do?"

"Helena," said Mother Michael decisively, "you must take this to the Lord in prayer. Go to the chapel, and ask God whether he will accept you."

Helena went immediately to the chapel, knelt, and prayed. At once she heard a voice telling her, "I accept you, for you are in my heart."

She rushed back to Mother Michael and repeated the response. Smiling, Mother said, "If the Lord has accepted you, then so shall I."

Mother Michael told the girl that, in her case, the congregation would waive the requirement for a dowry. Helena would need to bring only enough money to pay for her clothing in the convent, since the congregation had no funds for that purpose. The two sat down and worked out a plan for Helena to save part of her salary, bringing it periodically to the convent for safekeeping. When she had saved the entire amount, the Sisters of Our Lady of Mercy would gladly accept her.

Helena's heart was singing! She would continue working hard at her job with the Lipszyc family. *It will take about a year to save the money that I need,* she thought. *The time will fly by!*

While Helena worked and earned her wardrobe money, two complications arose. Mrs. Lipszyc, who was very fond of Helena, decided to try to find her a good husband. She had no idea about what was going on in the young woman's soul, and didn't believe that such an attractive young woman could really want to enter a convent! Helena was firm, however, and gently explained to her employer—and to the young men who came to visit the house—that she had pledged her life and heart to Jesus.

The other difficulty was a visit from her sister Josephine. She had been sent by Helena's parents in a last attempt to persuade her to come back home. The road to convent life wouldn't be easy, Helena realized, and she couldn't control what lay ahead for her. But she was sure of her vocation. No matter what happened, she would pursue a life with Jesus. Josephine went home alone.

6

CONVENT LIFE

On August 1, 1925, Helena walked down Zytnia Street and again knocked on the convent door. This time, her most ardent wish came true. She was accepted into the Congregation of the Sisters of Our Lady of Mercy.

Everything was new to Helena the postulant: the schedule, the faces that surrounded her, the prayers lifted up to the Lord in chapel. Helena realized that until now she had concentrated all her efforts on how to enter religious life but hadn't had much understanding of what the actual life would be like. As she learned the routines of community prayer, she understood how wonderful it was to have the opportunity to pray. She was no longer the little girl who could only go to Mass when it was her turn to wear the family dress. Now she rejoiced in attending Mass daily!

There was so much to learn. During classes on the history of the Sisters of Our Lady of Mercy, Helena listened eagerly. In

1818, a wealthy young woman named Thérèse Rondeau had founded the "House of Mercy" in Laval, France. Her mission was to take in and educate poor girls who were living on the streets, giving them a chance to reform their lives. The girls were given moral help and guidance. Mother Thérèse became the foundress of a religious congregation that grew rapidly. In 1862, Countess Eva Potocka founded a new religious congregation, the Sisters of Our Lady of Mercy, doing similar work with girls and women in Poland.

After just three weeks with the sisters, Helena began to face her first difficulties. *It's not at all the way I thought it would be,* she said to herself. *Why am I doing so much work? Where is all the prayer time I thought I would have?*

Helena was learning the many responsibilities of community service. Her duties might include laundry, cooking, washing dishes, and cleaning. Of course, the work took Helena longer because she was new. She was also very thorough, so she constantly felt that she was running out of time.

Other aspects of convent life were hard to adjust to as well. Now this young woman, who had always been spirited and lively, had to learn to walk slowly, speak in a quiet voice, speak only when she was spoken to, and pray at specified times. Life in the convent required adjustments from every postulant, but somehow Helena felt that she was struggling alone.

One evening she slipped into the small chapel, anxious for the chance to talk to Jesus. "Please tell me what you want me to do, dear Jesus. Should I leave this congregation in search of a cloistered order, one with more prayer time? Please tell me."

She waited. The Lord was silent. An uneasy feeling came over her. She felt all alone with her emptiness. Despite this, she told herself that she would approach Mother Superior about the matter after Mass the next morning.

Later, Helena made her way to the dormitory where she slept. She knelt by her bed in prayer. The lights were out and the other sisters were all asleep.

After remaining on her knees for a while, Helena lay on the floor, face down, and prayed. She sometimes did this when she was trying extra hard to communicate with

God. She begged to know his will. Suddenly, a light began to shine on the floor and on her bed. Helena saw the face of Jesus on one of the curtains that separated her bed from the beds on either side. Jesus was suffering and bloody. Tears slid silently down his cheeks and dropped onto her sheets. The young woman gasped.

"Jesus," she whispered, "who did this to you?"

"You are the one who will cause me this pain if you leave this convent. It is here that I called you, and I have prepared many graces for you."

Helena was stunned. She asked pardon, thanked Jesus, and got into bed. Finally, she felt peace. Here she had been called, and here she would stay.

Helena's days were spent in prayer, work, and study. She did everything as well and as thoroughly as she could. One of her assignments was kitchen duty. The other was to clean the room of Mother Jane, an elderly, ill sister. Helena loved being near Mother Jane, who was very holy. Mother Jane had once been postulant directress, and she was very kind to the young woman. "Helena is prayerful and spiritual," she told the other sisters.

The months passed and the superiors noticed that Helena was becoming physically weak. The young woman seemed so intense in her effort to be dedicated to her duties! For a while, she was given an easier assignment: she would be cooking in the congregation's small summer cottage. The daily schedule would allow for prayer and some extra rest. When she arrived at the cottage, Helena prepared supper for two other sisters and herself. As she worked, she prayed. "Jesus," she asked, "what especially would you like me to pray for while I am here?"

Jesus answered her in her heart: "I will let you know tomorrow night."

The next evening, Jesus answered through Helena's guardian angel, who revealed a brief vision of purgatory. Helena was standing in the midst of it, holding tightly to her angel's hand. She asked what the greatest sufferings of the souls in purgatory consisted of. They answered that the greatest torment was in wanting to be with God. Then Helena saw the Mother of God visiting and consoling the holy souls, and it was time to leave. Her angel led her away. She heard Jesus say, "This is not in the interests of mercy, but of justice."

Helena understood that the suffering souls in purgatory, longing for God, could not help themselves. She could help them, though, with her prayers and sacrifices. As the days passed, she prayed with love and fervor for all those in purgatory. She realized that the phrase "poor souls" had special meaning. These souls were rich because they were saved. They were poor, though, because they knew who God was and couldn't yet be with him. Helena was determined to use her prayers and sacrifices to help speed them on their way to heaven.

The days at the little cottage soon came to an end. Helena's health seemed better. She went to Kraków to join the group of postulants completing their last three months of training. The Sisters of Our Lady of Mercy ran a large school there for troubled young women. The postulants helped with various duties as they readied themselves to become novices, the next step in their vocational journey.

7

A New Name

Helena and her classmates began to look forward to life as novices. First of all, though, they would have to adjust to their new location. The school in Kraków where they now lived had a large enrollment. The buildings were surrounded by orchards and gardens cared for by the sisters. The grounds were beautiful, and the fruits and vegetables were important for their daily meals. The postulants would be a big help as groundskeepers.

The professed sisters who worked and taught at the school were all happy to be there. The school and grounds were known as Joseph's Place. All the sisters believed that Saint Joseph was watching over them with special love.

Helena adjusted easily to her pleasant life at Joseph's Place. Her final months as a postulant passed quickly. Helena and her companions made an eight-day retreat before they began their novitiate. This special time gave each of the young women the opportunity to listen and talk to God in prayer. It enabled them to meditate on the meaning of their lives, on their faith in God, and on their calling to be sisters.

On April 30, 1926, Helena and her co-novices received their religious habits and veils. A professed sister was assigned to help each novice put on her new items of clothing. Sister Clemens Buczek was Helena's helper. While Helena was putting on the habit, she suddenly received an inner message from Jesus. It lasted only a moment. The young sister saw vividly the sufferings she would be asked to bear throughout her life for Jesus' love.

It seemed for a moment that Helena was about to faint. Sister Clemens ran for the smelling salts. In that short time, Helena recovered and again became her normal self. The piercing pain and sadness were followed by peace and serenity.

Sister Clemens was confused. "Oh, you're just afraid you'll miss the pleasures of this world," the sister joked good-natured-ly. From then on, she occasionally teased Helena about the strange incident. Only after Helena's death did Sister Clemens find out what had really happened that day.

Sister Faustina suddenly saw the sufferings she would be asked to bear for the love of Jesus.

Finally, the moment had arrived. *I'm so excited,* Helena thought to herself. *This is all so new. Yet it's as if I've always been waiting for this wonderful day. If only Mama and Papa could be here to share my joy!*

Along with the religious habit and white veil, each novice received a new name. Helena listened intently as the priest pronounced hers: Maria Faustina. In the congregation, she would be known from then on simply as Sister Faustina. She repeated it happily over and over in her mind. *The name just seems to belong to me,* she thought to herself. *After all, Faustina means "blessed, fortunate one!"* "It's true," the novice said aloud, "I really am blessed and with Jesus I can only be happy." Softly she added, "Even if he allows some trials to come my way."

Novitiate training would take two years. The young sisters had classes on the Catholic faith, on religious life, and on the Rule of their order. They learned about spirituality, prayer, and centering their lives on the examples of Jesus in the Gospels. During brief times of relaxation together with Sister Mary Joseph, their director, the novices became better acquainted with each other.

Sister Placida, a co-novice, playfully called Sister Faustina "the theologian." She tried to stay near Sister Faustina to listen to her uplifting conversations. On nice days, when the novices could get together outside, Sister Faustina was at her best. She would lift her hands and pray, "O God, your works are so marvelous." There was such a contagious joy about her!

The novices helped in the kitchen, where there was a great deal of work to be done between prayer time and classes. Each took on various kitchen tasks for a week at a time.

Sister Faustina began to dread taking her turn at one task in particular. In her imagination she could see the huge pot on the stove filled with boiling potatoes. It seemed to her it would be impossible to tip the pot so that the hot water could pour out and steam could escape without spilling the potatoes.

She approached the novice director and asked, "Do you think I could be excused from a turn? I can't do it. I'll lose half the potatoes!" Sister Mary Joseph smiled. "Don't worry," she said kindly. "You'll learn how to do it well with practice." That wasn't the answer the novice had hoped for, but she knew she had to accept it.

Finally, she took the problem to Jesus. "I'm sorry I'm so weak," the young woman prayed. "Please help me."

As she continued to kneel in prayer, she heard Jesus' voice in her heart. "I will make this task easy for you, Faustina. I will strengthen you."

The novice went happily into the kitchen that night to help prepare supper. She headed straight for the large pot. She picked it up by the handles, protected from the heat by heavy potholders. Slowly, easily, she tipped the pot. The hot water poured off without a problem. She lifted the lid to let the steam escape and stared. Instead of potatoes, she saw fresh, beautiful roses in the pot! Sister Faustina stood rooted to the spot.

This is unbelievable! she whispered to herself.

Then, Jesus spoke in her heart and said: "I change all of your hard work into lovely flowers. Their perfume will reach the heavens." The novice was speechless. She smiled and thanked the Lord.

After that, Sister Faustina volunteered to help the other novices whenever it was their turn to handle the large pot of potatoes. She always trusted that Jesus would make her task possible.

8

CHALLENGES

Sister Faustina pronounced her religious vows of poverty, chastity, and obedience on April 30, 1928. To her great joy, her parents were able to travel from Glogowiec for the ceremony. They had come still hoping to persuade her to return home with them. But when they saw her happiness and fulfillment in the religious life, they finally understood. Their daughter really did belong to Jesus.

Sister Faustina remained in the convent at Kraków until October of that year. Her new home was the motherhouse on Zytnia Street in Warsaw. There, her life as a professed sister unfolded a day at a time. *I feel loved by Jesus, and so joyful,* the young sister thought. *I think Jesus is also pleased with me*, she smiled to herself. She performed her tasks happily. She began to understand the beauty of her vocation and lived each day with a peaceful heart. But almost at once, the young sister became ill and had to spend over a month at the infirmary.

Unfortunately, a few of the sisters who had never known Faustina were skeptical about her illness. "She acts as if she's so pious," someone remarked. "She's probably just looking for a little extra attention," added another. Several sisters began to circulate the rumor that she wasn't really sick, and began to watch her and to criticize what she said and did.

Sister Faustina was aware of these unkind attitudes. She never answered back or complained. Instead, she offered these difficulties to her Lord. "Jesus," Faustina whispered, "please help me."

"Don't worry," she heard in her heart. "You are not living for yourself, but for people who will profit from all your sufferings. What you suffer will give them light and courage to accept my will for them."

Sometimes Jesus spoke to Faustina about Poland. She began to pray every day that her beloved country could be spared times of suffering. She knew that World War I had cost Poland great loss of life. It had also cost hunger, homelessness, and grief. What could she do to bring God's protection and blessing on her country?

"Pray fervently at Mass," Jesus told her. "Offer my blood and wounds to my Father to make up for sins. Do this at Mass for seven days." Sister Faustina did this willingly.

On the seventh day, she saw Jesus on a cloud. "Please, Jesus," Faustina begged, "spare my country more pain and suffering. Have mercy on us all."

Jesus gazed at Faustina and smiled. "Please," she said, "bless me."

"For your sake," the Lord said, "I now bless the entire country." From his place in the clouds, Jesus traced a large sign of the cross over Poland.

In the following months, Sister Faustina was sent to live at various convents. She often filled in for sisters who would be away on short assignments of two or three months. Faustina was probably chosen for frequent transfers because she, unlike some of the other sisters, never complained about it. She made the best of any situation. In each new location, she would generally be assigned to the kitchen. Physically, though, the work was often too hard. In between assignments, the superiors sometimes sent her to one of their smaller summer homes for rest and lighter duties.

Early in 1931, Sister Faustina was living in the large convent in the city of Plock. On the evening of February 22, when she was about to go to bed, Jesus appeared to her as the living image of the merciful God. He was dressed in a white robe. His right hand was raised in blessing, and his left hand was over his heart. Two bright rays, one red and one pale, streamed from the area of his heart.

Then Jesus spoke. "Paint an image just like this, with the line 'Jesus, I trust in you.' This image should be venerated first in your chapel, and then throughout the whole world." Jesus also asked for an annual Feast of Divine Mercy to be celebrated on the Sunday after Easter.

When Jesus had finished speaking, the vision disappeared. Sister Faustina spent the rest of that night praying and wondering. *What can this mean? How can I paint the image of the merciful Jesus? I'm no artist!* The young sister felt like running and hiding. *Why does Jesus want me to do this? Who will listen to me? No one outside of the convent even knows me, except my family. I have no influence on anyone. Even some of the sisters I live with don't accept or understand me.*

Finally, though, all her fears were washed away by the knowledge that she was to be the messenger of Jesus, bringing his divine mercy to the whole world. Faustina was his choice, and she was overjoyed. Jesus said softly in her heart, "I will expect many people to be saved because of this devotion."

Sister Faustina didn't know how it would all come to be, but she did know that, somehow, she would carry out the will of her Lord. After all, what were the words he had told her to inscribe under his image?

"Jesus, I trust in you."

And Faustina did.

The seasons of the Church's liturgy passed by: Advent, Christmas, Lent, Easter.

Jesus spoke to Faustina about spreading the devotion to the Divine Mercy to priests. Faustina understood that this was so they could share it with all the people of their parishes. But how could she get her message to priests? Faustina thought and prayed, trusting that the Lord would lead her.

In November 1932, Sister Faustina and her companions met in Warsaw to begin preparation for their final vows. Mother Margaret Gimbutt would direct them. In between classes, Sister Faustina would help another sister with sewing and mending the sisters' clothes.

The sister in charge wasn't at all enthusiastic about having Faustina as a helper. During the weeks ahead, Faustina became ill and had to ask her superior if she could go to bed. The sister she worked with thought she was lazy, and was quite unkind at times. Faustina was sorry to cause her companion such stress. She could only pray to Jesus to lighten the sister's burden.

Later that winter, Jesus gave Faustina a very special prayer. Jesus told her that by saying this prayer with faith and contrition on behalf of a sinner, the sinner would be given the grace of conversion.

The prayer Jesus gave her is this: "Oh Blood and Water, which gushed forth from the Heart of Jesus as a fount of mercy for us, I trust in You" (*Diary*, 84).

During Lent that year, Faustina experienced a vision of Jesus suffering his scourging at the pillar. She asked the priest during her confession if she could take on more penances. The priest agreed, and Faustina felt that Jesus was speaking through him.

One of the young women in the sisters' care was suffering thoughts of suicide. Faustina asked Jesus if she could take to herself the girl's temptations. Jesus agreed. Suddenly, Faustina felt powerfully drawn to discouragement and despair. Death seemed like a blessed escape from so much sadness. Sister Faustina understood firsthand what the young woman had been experiencing. Seven days of torture went by until the torment finally left her. The student, too, was in peace. Her thoughts of suicide were gone.

Faustina's own youngest sister, Wanda, who was thirteen years old, came to the convent for a visit, depressed and seeking comfort. The young woman stayed with the sisters for two weeks. Faustina offered prayers and sacrifices to Jesus. Her sister gradually became peaceful. Wanda went back home a happy young woman. Sister Faustina knew that, with the Lord's help, her prayers and sufferings had brought about a miracle.

9

HELP FROM HEAVEN

"Jesus, you know just what you want," Faustina smiled as she prayed. "It's so easy for you and so hard for me. I trust that you will make it all happen." But how would it happen? How could she make the whole world aware of the merciful Jesus from the quiet of the convent? What could she do to prepare herself to be more ready to do what Jesus would ask of her? She prayed, worked, and waited.

Her superiors invited her to make a thirty-day spiritual retreat. During the retreat, she went to confession to Father Andrasz, a Jesuit priest, who listened with his heart and gave her words of encouragement. Father Andrasz told her that she was on the right path and in God's hands. He also told her that she should not abandon her mission to have a painting made of the image of the merciful Jesus. Sister Faustina understood that she was to continue to trust in God and that all would be accomplished—in God's time.

Before Faustina knew it, the time had come for her to make her final vows as a religious sister. That day came on May 1, 1933. As she spoke the words that sealed her commitment as a Sister of Our Lady of Mercy, Sister Faustina's soul was filled with profound joy.

Soon Sister Faustina was on her way to a new assignment: her order's convent in Vilnius. *Will everything go well?* she wondered.

Her worries formed a prayer to Jesus. "Do not fear," the Lord said in her heart. "I will not leave you alone."

Sister Faustina's new community consisted of eighteen sisters and a number of students. The superior appointed Faustina chief gardener. Actually, she would be the only sister-gardener and would have some students as helpers during their free time. *I don't know a thing about gardening,* Faustina thought to herself, *but I'm willing to try my best!*

Fortunately, a missionary brother who lived near the convent was an expert gardener. By asking his advice, Faustina learned more than enough to begin her new duties. Soon the convent gardens and greenhouses were prospering.

Sister Faustina waited with the other sisters for confession. Father Andrasz wouldn't be there. He was back in Kraków. The words of Jesus came into her heart once more: "Do not fear, I will not leave you alone." Then she remembered a vision she had seen not too long before she came to Vilnius. She was in a church. A priest was standing for a moment between the altar and the confessional. She could see his face well enough to know that he was a stranger to her. That face came back to her now.

In her mind, she saw the priest just as clearly as she had then. When would she meet him? She was sure that he would be the next link in the chain of her mission to spread the message of Divine Mercy. Moments later, the priest arrived for confession. He knelt in prayer in the convent chapel. Then he turned and walked toward the confessional. Faustina saw his face clearly. It was the priest from her vision.

Sister Faustina approached the confessional with a smile. At last, her special assignment for Jesus would move ahead. The priest's name was Father Sopocko. The young sister confessed her sins and told of her visions. She also explained to Father simply and briefly that God had shown him to her as her future spiritual director.

The priest was silent for a few moments. Who was this sister? Was she really receiving messages from Jesus, or was she deluded and confused? Father Sopocko knew he would have to move slowly. He tested Faustina and questioned whether or not her reports were really true.

Faustina had never expected that. When her confession was over, she returned to her pew and said her penance. Then she thought, *I can't go back to him. He doesn't believe me. I'll find another confessor.* "*Jesus,*" she whispered in her heart, "*where are you now?*"

She went to a new confessor, Father Dabrowski, a Jesuit who was also doubtful about Faustina's experiences. This wasn't helping! Sister Faustina had to do something and, after all, Jesus had sent her a vision of Father Sopocko as her spiritual director. She returned to him in confession and told him that she would accept any test he felt was needed. Somehow, this time she found it easy to pour out her heart to the priest. Faustina realized that it was because this was what God wanted.

After several months of questioning and testing, Father Sopocko understood that

Sister Faustina really was a well-balanced person who truly had been gifted with special graces. Although Father Sopocko was a man of few words, he had begun to think seriously about the message of Divine Mercy. He began to realize that it would be necessary for him to cooperate in the great work of making it known.

Father Sopocko was an experienced spiritual director, and he guided Sister Faustina carefully. "You will suffer, Sister Faustina," he explained gently. "Some won't understand or even believe your message. They might judge you wrongly, but you must not lose heart. You know how important the Divine Mercy message is. It is meant for the entire world. So be strong. Many people will benefit from your courage and virtue."

Sister Faustina repeated to Father Sopocko the messages and visions just as Jesus had asked her to do. Jesus had explained to her in detail how he wanted the Divine Mercy image to look. Father Sopocko found a well-known local painter, Eugene Kazimierowski. The priest hired Kazimierowski to paint the image. Finally, the great work would move forward!

Every two weeks, Father Sopocko and Sister Faustina visited the painter in his studio. The artist worked as Sister gave instructions about the exact details of the picture. Father Sopocko sat quietly, taking notes. Jesus, Sister Faustina explained, had told her that the pale ray flowing from the area of his heart stood for the water of grace, which makes souls pure, and the red ray stood for blood, which is the life of the soul. It was very important to Faustina that every detail of the painting be correct.

Sister Faustina studied the painting carefully at every visit. She always felt happy and yet a little sad, too. Even the most skilled painter, she knew, could never truly, accurately represent the full glory of Jesus!

On the Sunday after Easter, Sister Faustina celebrated Divine Mercy Sunday, as Jesus had asked. She believed that some day the whole world would join her in this wonderful celebration. For now, however, she had to be patient and wait. All things would unfold in God's time!

The Divine Mercy painting was completed in June 1934. It was placed in a dark hallway of the convent of the Bernardine Sisters near Saint Michael's Church, where Father Sopocko was pastor.

Around that time, Father Sopocko asked Sister Faustina to begin keeping a diary of

"My grace makes the painting valuable," said Jesus.

her visions and spiritual visitations. Obediently, Faustina began. Neither of them had any idea how important this little diary would someday become to the whole world!

While Sister Faustina cared for the convent garden, a friend of hers from novitiate days worked in the kitchen. Sister Justine was the cook and dishwasher for the sisters. Often, when Faustina's gardening was done for the day, she would stop by the kitchen to help Sister Justine. Even though it was nearly bedtime, Sister Justine always had plenty of dishes and pots to wash. The two sisters would finish the chore together.

One day, when the cook had to go out, Sister Faustina was chosen to replace her. That evening, Justine returned home. She found her friend resting peacefully on a bench in the kitchen. The meal was finished as well as all the supper dishes. Everything was neat and clean.

"How did you do it all?" the astonished Sister Justine asked.

"Oh," Sister Faustina confided, "the angels came and helped me. I could never have done it by myself."

10

BACK TO GLOGOWIEC

One hot summer evening, the Blessed Mother appeared to Sister Faustina. Mary's voice and manner were gentle and calm. "You will soon suffer an illness," the Blessed Virgin explained. "You will also suffer because of the Divine Mercy painting."

Faustina thought about the message. She soon became ill. The convent doctor didn't correctly diagnose Sister Faustina's sickness. He told her superiors she was suffering from a bad cold. In reality, her illness would prove to be much more serious.

As the days passed, she felt sick much of the time. She asked Jesus for the strength to be brave and faithful to the duties of her daily life. On Thursday, August 9, 1934, Sister Faustina remembered that the sisters would be taking turns making Hours of Adoration throughout the night. She would add her name to the list. During this special time, Faustina prayed that sinners would find sorrow for the way they lived. She prayed that they would have the courage to give up evil habits and live holy lives. She prayed for people who had lost hope in Jesus and his merciful love. She prayed for ungrateful people, that they would become loving and thankful to Jesus for all his gifts. The Hour of Adoration, from eleven until midnight, passed quickly.

The next sister came to the chapel. It was time for Faustina to leave. When she was halfway to her bedroom, Faustina felt a strange presence. It was as if something or someone was crowding her. Suddenly, there was so much noise that Sister Faustina wanted to cover her ears. She realized, though, that she was the only one who could hear the growls and howling of a pack of demons that looked like dogs.

"You are stealing people away from us," one of them threatened. "We'll tear you to shreds!"

Faustina kept walking calmly to her bedroom. "I'm not afraid of you," she responded. Whispering softly, she prayed, "Jesus, my merciful God, will protect me."

"Let's get out of here!" one of the demons shouted. "She isn't alone. God is with her." Then they were gone, and Sister Faustina was soon peacefully asleep.

Three days later, on August 12, Faustina became very ill. Father Sopocko administered the sacrament of the Anointing of the Sick as the sister gasped for air. The doctor came and gave her medicine that helped her breathe more easily. The terrible sensation of suffocating became less frightening. As soon as she had a small amount of relief, though, the devils were there in her room, taunting her.

The next day Faustina was well enough to go to Mass. As she received Jesus in the Holy Eucharist, she said, "I thought you were going to take me, Lord."

Jesus explained in her heart, "I am pleased with your trust, but your love should be even stronger. I want you to unite your own sufferings to my sufferings on the cross."

One day in October, Sister Faustina and some of the students were leaving the garden to go to supper. Suddenly, the merciful Jesus appeared to her in the sky above the chapel! The two rays, one pale and one red, covered the chapel, the infirmary, and then spread to cover the whole city—and the world. Only Sister Faustina saw Jesus, but Imelda, one of the students, could see the two rays.

"My goodness!" the girl gasped. She tried to explain the scene to the others, but they saw nothing. Imelda, however, persisted. Sister Faustina was asked to write a statement regarding the vision. Imelda confirmed her account, and the superior of the house, Mother Irene, authenticated it. Sister Faustina wasn't happy about the attention this brought her, but she rejoiced that Jesus was making himself known. "For the sake of Jesus," she declared, "I can bear anything."

Soon it was time for the convent's annual February retreat. Sister Faustina felt well enough to rejoice in the peace and joy of her religious life during the eight days. Soon after, though, she received word from her family that her mother had become very ill and was close to death. Sister Faustina was deeply saddened. She asked for and obtained permission to travel back to her family home in Glogowiec, 250 miles away.

The following night, as Sister Faustina climbed from the taxi she had taken from the train station, the lights of the little cottage glowed softly through the small windows. Snow was piled along the sides of the lane, and she could hear the cattle mooing softly in the barn nearby. Home! Faustina's hands were shaking as she lifted her small satchel and stepped toward the door, her shoes crunching on the snow.

The visit was her first and only visit to the family she loved so much. Medicines hadn't done much good for the ailing Marianna Kowalska, but the presence of her beloved daughter proved to be the best medicine of all. The next day, Sunday, the entire family went to Mass together, even Mama. "As soon as I saw Helena, I got well!" she informed another daughter.

After Mass, it was time for a family meal. Faustina looked at each of her family members with wonder. Her parents had gotten so much older. Her brothers and sisters were adults. "You've all grown up," Faustina said softly. "So much is changed and yet so much is the same. I've missed you all very much."

"And we've missed you!" came the chorus. Everyone took turns at cooking. Faustina was asked to tell stories of the saints over and over again. The entire family joined in singing hymns. Several who had brought musical instruments provided a joyous accompaniment with their violins and mandolins.

The days of Sister Faustina's visit passed quickly. Every morning, her brother, Stanislaus, walked with her to Mass. Kneeling in the small, quiet church, Faustina prayed for all of her family. Two of her sisters couldn't come home for her visit. "I fear that they are in spiritual danger," she prayed to Jesus. "Please protect them." Within her heart, Jesus promised that he would give Faustina's sisters not only necessary graces, but special graces, too.

Soon the neighbors found out that the little girl they had known as Helena had come for a visit. They had to see her. What was her name now? Sister Faustina? How lovely. Mothers started to come with their babies and toddlers. "Please, a blessing for my child," they would say. "Please give my child a hug."

Faustina smiled and then laughed. It had been a long time since she had seen so many little children in that yard. They touched the rosary beads at her side and looked up eagerly at her for a smile and a greeting. Sister's visit was a special occasion for these country families. Many of them had never seen a religious sister in person and perhaps would never see another one. Sister Faustina gave many hugs and kisses to the little ones!

All too soon it was time to return to the convent. Papa, Mama, and Faustina's godparents each kissed and blessed her. The whole family was crying. "We pray that you will always be faithful to God's graces," said Papa. "And may you always remember and be grateful for God's goodness in calling you to religious life."

Faithful Stanislaus walked his sister to the waiting car. "God loves you and cares for you," Faustina said softly to her brother. Suddenly, overcome by emotion, he burst into tears. Sister Faustina patted him affectionately and got into the car. Only when she was out of sight did she break down and sob.

Faustina was never to see her parents again. In fact, they would outlive her. Her father lived to be seventy-eight. Her mother died many years later at the age of ninety.

11

JESUS' SPECIAL REQUEST

During the days of Lent in 1935, in her heart, Sister Faustina walked along the way of the cross with Jesus. She could imagine his terrible pain. *That is what Lent is all about,* she thought. *We, who sin, have our sins paid for by Jesus, our merciful Savior. Imagine if people really understood what our sins cost our Savior.* Sister Faustina wanted to do so much more to help people see, really see, the price of our salvation.

The convent was quiet on Good Friday. At 3:00 PM, Sister Faustina walked into the chapel. As she moved toward a pew, she heard Jesus' voice clearly: "I wish the image to be publicly honored." Faustina also had a clear vision of Jesus, close to death, with the red and pale rays radiating.

Soon, after prayer and meditation, Sister Faustina was able to talk to her spiritual director, Father Sopocko. Jesus had told her that a three-day celebration, a triduum, had been planned for the closing of the Jubilee Year of the Redemption at the famous *Ostra*

Brama, the Shrine of Our Lady of the Dawn. It was here that Jesus wanted the painting to be hung. "Please, Father," Faustina begged, "help me to fulfill Jesus' wish."

Faustina was firm in her insistence that the Divine Mercy painting must hang for three days at the shrine during the weekend of the first Sunday after Easter. Father Sopocko was a gentle, quiet man. Upon hearing Faustina's request, however, he was beside himself with worry. His mind raced. Was there really a celebration scheduled at the shrine? If so, the ceremonies must have been planned for months. How on earth could he influence the authorities to include this additional element? How could he even explain his request—straight from Jesus— to the priest in charge of the shrine? What if he said no?

Sister Faustina stood by quietly while Father Sopocko struggled. Suddenly, it occurred to him that the Sunday of the Jubilee celebration was the first Sunday after Easter: Mercy Sunday. Jesus' plans were falling into place! The priest turned to Faustina and said, "This is clearly the will of our Lord. I'll try my best. I'll go right now to the shrine and ask."

The three-day celebration was indeed to take place. Sister Faustina's information had been accurate. Father Zawadzki, the pastor of the shrine, even invited Father Sopocko to preach the homilies. Father Sopocko responded, "I'll preach the homilies if you give me permission to hang the Divine Mercy painting throughout the celebration." Father Zawadzki had to check with the archbishop, who said yes. The Divine Mercy painting was displayed on Thursday evening and hung until Monday.

On Friday, April 26, 1935, Father Sopocko preached a wonderful homily on divine mercy. While he was speaking, Sister Faustina gazed up at the painting. To her adoring eyes, the image came alive. The grace of God's mercy flowed over the worshippers, many of whom sensed a special power and beauty emanating from the painting. What did it all mean? Who was responsible for this lovely artwork?

Sister Faustina was questioned by the sisters of her own congregation as well as by people who attended the Jubilee celebrations. She hadn't received permission from her superiors or her spiritual director to reveal the truth of her communications with

Jesus, so of course, she couldn't speak of them. It was difficult to answer the questions without lying—but without telling the whole truth, either! Some of her own sisters were suspicious of poor Faustina. To them, this just confirmed their belief that she was putting herself forward, pretending to be special.

"Oh, her," went the whispers, "she thinks she's so holy!" Fortunately, not everyone felt that way, and Sister Faustina's superiors knew the truth.

When the celebrations had ended, the Divine Mercy painting was taken back to Father Sopocko's parish. For now, it was returned to the dark hallway of the Bernardine Sisters' convent.

During the summer of 1935, Sister Faustina was increasingly aware of the remaining challenges of her mission to make the Divine Mercy message known. More and more, she understood that she was united with Jesus to pray for, and suffer for, the souls of others. During that summer, she worked hard in the garden and even harder to do God's will.

On the evening of September 13, 1935, Sister Faustina went wearily to her little bedroom. She was exhausted at the end of each day of work, and she coughed frequently. How much longer would her health hold out?

Suddenly, an angel appeared to her, and Faustina had a clear vision of God in heaven. She felt, in her soul, the power of Jesus' grace. A wonderful new prayer, asking God to have mercy on the world, came into her heart.

The next day, as she entered the chapel, Jesus spoke to her once again. She learned more about the prayer and understood exactly how the Lord wished it to be prayed. This prayer, the Chaplet of Divine Mercy, was to be shared with her community and with the whole world. (You will find the Chaplet of Divine Mercy on page 111 of this book.)

By the end of October, Sister Faustina understood clearly that Jesus wanted his divine mercy celebrated with a feast day every year on the first Sunday after Easter. He also wanted the Divine Mercy painting to be moved from the convent to the church where Father Sopocko was pastor. Filled with trust in Jesus, Sister Faustina no longer worried about how she would accomplish these things. After all, wasn't it in the hands of the Lord? He could do anything; Faustina was merely his messenger. She offered her prayer of thanksgiving that God was allowing her to cooperate in giving this wonderful devotion to the world.

In March 1936, Faustina received the news that she would be leaving Vilnius for the congregation's convent in Warsaw. Two unusual things happened before her departure. An elderly sister approached her near the chapel door. "Sister Faustina," she said softly, clutching Faustina's hand, "I want to ask a special favor of you."

"Of course," Faustina responded, as she looked into the sister's tear-filled eyes. "How can I help?"

"Please ask Jesus to answer my question. I know that you are very close to him." The sister had been struggling spiritually for several years, worrying about whether or not Jesus had forgiven her sins. During Benediction of the Blessed Sacrament that evening, Faustina asked Jesus for an answer. In her soul, she heard: "Tell her that her disbelief hurts me more than the sins she has committed." After prayers, Faustina went to the elderly sister and repeated the answer just as Jesus had given it. The sister clasped her hands over her mouth in wonder. Tears of relief and joy slid down her cheeks.

The next morning, as Sister Faustina was preparing to leave for the train station, another sister approached her. "I have a confession to make," she said meekly. "I don't know if you noticed it, but I deliberately tried to annoy you many times. I was spiteful and jealous. I'm sorry, Sister Faustina." Faustina smiled.

Oh, yes, she said to herself, *I noticed it.*

Aloud, she said simply, "Of course I forgive you, Sister."

12

TOWARD THE GOAL

In the order's large convent in Warsaw, Sister Faustina's daily work made her very tired. This in turn made her medical condition worse. A few weeks after Easter in 1936, the superiors sent her to a smaller convent in the country to recover. She appreciated this and was doubly happy to have the company of her friend, Sister Justine. On one occasion, just before Faustina was to return to Warsaw, the two sisters had a brief but special conversation.

"Sister Justine," Faustina said gently, "I want to share a secret with you, a joyful secret, because I treasure you as a very dear friend."

"Oh, yes, Sister Faustina," her friend said.

"I know when I'm going to die," said Faustina with a faint trace of a smile. Her friend's eyes brimmed with tears, but she remained silent.

"Jesus has told me that I will die two years from now, in October of 1938. I know that when I leave here in a few minutes, I won't be seeing you again on this earth." Looking at the pain in her friend's eyes, she added: "We'll be together with Jesus someday, dear Sister Justine. Pray for me, and I will do the same for you. Just one more thing: please keep our conversation a secret while I am still alive."

Sister Justine stood waving as the car drove away. She hoped that Sister Faustina couldn't see her tears.

The weeks and months of 1936 passed. Sister Faustina was delighted to see a brochure on the devotion to Divine Mercy written and published by Father Sopocko. It was at this time that he told her that he would also print a holy card. The card would have the picture of the merciful Jesus on the front and the Divine Mercy prayer on the back. Now many more people would learn about this treasure.

Meanwhile, Faustina became frailer and frailer. She was sent to a lung specialist, who finally gave her illness a name: tuberculosis. In Faustina's time, before modern medications were available, tuberculosis always led to death. The doctor explained that Sister Faustina should be separated from the other sisters to keep the disease from spreading. She was moved to the infirmary section of the convent but, once again, some of the sisters didn't understand or believe in her illness. In spite of the doctor's instructions that she was to have complete rest and isolation, she wasn't getting either.

"Oh, the doctor is just saying you're so sick because he wants you to rest," one sister told her. "The best thing for you would be to get up and get working!"

Sister Faustina didn't really understand much about her illness, but she fully understood the pain it caused her—physically, from the tuberculosis, and emotionally, from the lack of understanding of some of her sisters. Whenever she felt agonizing suffering, she would turn her attention to Jesus and his mercy. Her strength would come from him, she believed with all her heart.

On December 9, 1936, Sister Chrysostom drove Faustina to a sanatorium, a special hospital designed to help tuberculosis patients. It was located a little over six miles outside the city of Kraków. Faustina was greeted at the door by a kindly young doctor, Adam Silberg. He had diagnosed her illness a few months before and was glad to welcome her among his patients.

Her treatment would take about three months.

Sister Faustina had heard Jesus in her heart before she had left the convent telling her not to worry, for he would be going with her. A nurse led her to a private room and helped her to feel at home. Faustina felt sick all the next day, but the day after that, Friday, she was able to go to Mass.

During that night, Sister Faustina woke from time to time, trying to get used to her new surroundings. Once she awoke suddenly, sure she had heard a call for help. She listened. No sound came, but she had the strongest sense that someone was in need of her prayers. "Dear Jesus," she prayed, "please help the person who is in need." Then she drifted off to sleep.

The next morning, Sister Faustina was told that a lady in the woman's ward was dying. Faustina felt that it must have been that person who had called for her help during the night. She got up and made her way quietly to the bedside of the woman. She knelt down and said the Divine Mercy Chaplet on her rosary beads. The words were loving and comforting.

As Faustina repeated the prayer over and over on her beads, the woman opened her eyes and looked directly at her. Before Sister Faustina had finished saying the chaplet, the woman died peacefully. Jesus told Sister Faustina in her heart that the woman's soul had been saved. This woman was the first person known to be saved through the powerful Chaplet of Divine Mercy.

Three weeks passed. Each time a priest came to hear the confessions of the patients, Sister Faustina was unavailable, sometimes because of a doctor's appointment, sometimes because of medical tests. She really felt the need to receive the sacrament of Reconciliation. Tears filled her eyes and flowed down her cheeks.

That afternoon, to her joy, Father Andrasz came into her room and sat down on a chair next to her bed. He invited her to confess. Sister Faustina named each fault and sin slowly, with great care. Father replied to each one. For her penance, he asked her to recite the Litany of the Holy Name of Jesus, which was in Faustina's prayer book. The priest rose from his chair and raised his right arm to absolve her from her sins. As he pronounced the words, a bright light came from him and Sister gasped. It was not Father Andrasz, but Jesus! Brilliant light shone all around him.

"Oh, Jesus," Sister Faustina exclaimed, "you heard my confession. I'm overwhelmed!" The room was silent now and the sister quietly performed the penance that Jesus had chosen for her.

On December 23, Sister Chrysostom came to visit Sister Faustina. She brought apples, lemons, and a little Christmas tree. The patient welcomed her visitor with love and gratitude. She appreciated the gifts, too.

Sister Chrysostom talked to Doctor Silberg. "Mother Superior would be so grateful if you would let us take Sister Faustina to our Warsaw convent for Christmas," Sister said. The kind doctor was very happy with the idea. He knew this would do his patient more good than all the medicine in the world. They arranged to have Sister Cajetan come to take Faustina to Warsaw. She would return to the sanatorium after Christmas.

13

THE STRANGER

Sister Faustina's hospital stay had to be extended beyond three months. She took the change of plans calmly. After all, Jesus was with her in all of this. Soon it was mid-February 1937. Snow and wind isolated the sanatorium, but Faustina never felt lonely. Her heart reached out, first to the other patients, and then to the world beyond the snowdrifts. Today she wanted to help sinners. She picked up her crochet hook and yarn. "This is how I will help all those in need." She began to crochet and prayed: "Dear Jesus, please grant conversion to as many people as the number of stitches I make today with this hook."

Jesus answered in her heart: "You are asking too much. This also requires some sacrifice for each person who is granted such a grace." Faustina thought for a moment. Jesus was telling her that she would also have to do penance for each sinner. She could only offer small penances from her hospital room.

"Jesus, please accept my little penances, just as every stitch from my crochet hook, as if they were great."

"Yes," Jesus answered in her soul, "I will do as you ask."

One night later that spring, Sister Faustina learned that a certain young man was dying.

Someone is in pain and near death, she thought. Faustina started to pray the Chaplet of Divine Mercy. She prayed the entire chaplet for the young man, but he continued to suffer terribly, moaning pitifully. Faustina heard a voice within her say: "Pray the chaplet again." She understood then that the young man was in urgent need of extra prayers.

Faustina locked herself in her room, lay on the floor, face down, and again prayed the chaplet, begging Jesus for mercy for the poor man. Then she thought of the crucifix she wore around her neck. She had received it when she had pronounced her first vows as a religious sister. She took the crucifix off.

What happened next is not totally clear. Although Sister Faustina probably did not physically leave her room, it seems that she was spiritually present in the room of the young man, who was dying in great pain. She laid the crucifix gently on the young man's chest. His breathing became peaceful and he no longer tossed and turned. He died peacefully.

"How much we should pray for those who are dying," Faustina whispered to Jesus. "Your mercy remains a fountain of water that can quench people thirsting to be saved."

Late in March, Sister Faustina was released from the sanatorium. Her tuberculosis advanced as the months of 1937 passed by. She was very frail, and her job was changed from gardener to gatekeeper. She was put in charge of answering the door and welcoming the many poor people who came to the convent seeking food. These were hard times for her fellow countrymen, who were as hardworking as her own parents had always been. Sister Faustina opened the gate and offered her gentle smile and kind greeting. Some came more than once. She recognized them but never let them feel that they were unwelcome.

The September winds were brisk and leaves were falling from the trees one midmorning when Faustina opened the gate. A young man stood there, his eyes sad and hungry. The sister smiled and greeted him kindly. He shivered as the winds whipped by.

"May I have something to eat, Sister?" he asked.

"Oh yes," Faustina said. "Please wait here. I'll just be a moment."

The entrance to the convent blocked the winds and the young man felt a bit more comfortable. Sister Faustina went quickly to the kitchen. Nothing had been set aside for the poor that day. Finally, she found some soup and heated it over the open fire of the kitchen stove. She crumpled up bread into the soup to make it more filling, and then hurried down the hallway toward the door. She handed the soup to the stranger. It was quickly gone. As she reached to take the mug back, she looked into the stranger's young face. "Jesus," she gasped. "It's really you!"

In an instant he was gone.

As Faustina returned to her post at the gate, she heard Jesus speaking in her heart: "The poor are thanking me because I sent you to them," he said.

The wind softened and the sun shone bright as Faustina continued her duties with a peaceful heart.

"Jesus!" Faustina gasped. "It's really you!"

14

YOU *ARE* A SAINT

Advent and Christmas passed by. Faustina's illness slowly advanced, but she remained serene. Over and over, she thought about the words of Jesus. Even though her pain increased, she felt joy.

Because her illness wasn't understood, the sister in charge of the infirmary neglected Sister Faustina. At times, Faustina's throat was parched, but her water pitcher was empty and remained that way for what seemed like hours at a time. Another sister was assigned to clean Faustina's room, but she rarely did it for fear of catching her disease. Meanwhile, Faustina prayed to be patient and kind. Some days she felt anxious for heaven. She knew that Jesus would soon be coming to take her to paradise.

By the end of January 1938, Sister Faustina felt strong enough to go to the dining room with the sisters for her meals. To fill the long hours, she kept busy praying and crocheting lace that would be sewn onto altar linens.

One day as she sewed silently, her lips moving in prayer, she asked Jesus in her heart: "May I tell you about something that is bothering me?"

"Of course," Jesus replied.

"For as long as I have been in the order, a few sisters have called me a saint, in an accusing way. I know that they are making fun of me and I feel very bad about it." Sister Faustina waited to hear Jesus' reply.

Jesus said: "Is this what you are sad about? Faustina, you *are* a saint. In a short time I will show the whole world that this is true. Those who make fun of you will call you that same word, saint, but then they will really mean it."

As Sister Faustina's illness advanced, her sufferings became unbearable. She offered the pain for all those who would be touched by the devotion to Divine Mercy. "Before the day of justice," Jesus said, "I am sending the day of mercy."

Little by little, some of the sisters began to recognize the holiness of Sister Faustina. They would ask her to pray for special intentions. She willingly did this. Her friend, Sister Amelia Socha, also had tuberculosis. Hers was in the bones. Sister Amelia whispered to her friend, "I'm so afraid to be a burden to the community. Please ask Jesus to give me the grace of an early death."

Sister Faustina responded kindly, "My friend, Jesus wants you to know that you will die a year after me."

As 1938 progressed, both Sister Faustina and Sister Amelia treasured each day as a gift. Sister Faustina knew that she would not live until the end of the year. She was driven to the sanatorium so that Doctor Silberg could monitor her illness and prescribe medications. The visits were tiring and, most of all, she felt terrible thirst. When Mother Superior stopped by her room, she was worried.

"We have to do something," she said. "You need regular treatments. Things just can't go on this way." Faustina didn't respond. Instead, she was thinking to herself: *All I really want at the moment is water in my pitcher,* but she didn't want to bother anybody.

Soon it was Holy Week, and then Easter. Sister Faustina celebrated in her heart the Feast of the Divine Mercy, believing that some day this powerful devotion would spread throughout the world and would be celebrated gloriously on the Sunday after Easter. On April 21, Faustina was taken back to the sanatorium at Pradnik. She was relieved to find Doctor Silberg and the staff of sisters who served the patients so lovingly. Faustina settled in her bed and drifted off to sleep.

The next morning, the patient prayed and prepared at least to receive Jesus spiritually in her heart. She hoped that when she began to feel better, she would be able to really receive the Holy Eucharist.

Suddenly she saw a flash of light, and blinked. An angel stood at the end of her bed. He wore a gold cape and carried a crystal chalice. The angel approached her, held up the Host, and said, "Behold the Lord of Angels." He placed the Eucharist gently on her tongue.

The angel came to Sister Faustina every day for nearly two weeks. Once Sister Faustina asked, "Could you please hear my confession?"

"No spirit in heaven is able to do that," the angel replied. Just then, the Host left the angel's hands and came to rest on Sister Faustina's tongue.

Days and weeks passed. Sometime late in June, Sister Faustina became so weak that she could no longer lift her pen to write in her diary. But her courage and her faith in Jesus' mercy continued, stronger than ever.

15

THE LONG ROAD HOME

The humid heat of summer hung heavily, like a thick blanket, over the hospital rooms. The staff called Mother Irene and explained that Sister Faustina's condition was growing more serious. Mother Irene rushed to the hospital and remained by her bedside throughout the day. Sister Faustina had a painful night and awoke on a new day—August 25, 1938. It was her thirty-third birthday. The chaplain gave her the Anointing of the Sick. Often, this sacrament brings physical as well as spiritual healing. Faustina's health did not seem to improve, but she lingered peacefully. Her time at the hospital was now ended. The doctors could do no more for her. On September 17, one of the sisters of her congregation, Sister Alfreda, came to bring her home to the convent.

"I'm going to miss you, Sister Faustina," Doctor Silberg said. "You've helped me so much in my newfound Catholic faith. All my questions...you always took time no matter how sick you felt. Thank you."

Doctor Silberg went over to the small nightstand and picked up the holy card of Saint Thérèse of Lisieux that belonged to Sister Faustina.

"Sister," the doctor asked simply, "may I please have this? I have a six-year-old son. I would like to frame this picture and hang it over his bed."

"Certainly," Faustina said with a smile.

"Oh, Doctor, be careful," Sister Alfreda said. "Maybe you should disinfect the card first."

The doctor smiled. "I'm not afraid of contamination," he said. "I believe that Sister Faustina is a saint, and saints do not contaminate."

The frail Sister Faustina was carried out to the car and gently seated inside.

"I'm so happy that I'll die at the convent," Faustina said softly.

"Oh, please, Sister, don't die right now, in the car," Sister Alfreda gasped. "What will I do?"

"Don't worry," Sister Faustina told her calmly. "I won't die today. It's not time yet."

The car moved ahead, and Sister Alfreda tried to avoid the bumps and potholes. Soon they were home. Sister Faustina's private room was clean and inviting. The sister caring for the sick at that time was Sister Amelia. A kind and gentle soul, she did everything possible to make her patient more comfortable.

Sister Faustina was so grateful. She wished she could eat something, since Sister Amelia prepared her trays so carefully. But she could no longer find the strength to swallow. Her lips moved in prayer. She was at peace. Father Sopocko came for a short visit on September 22. He came again four days later, his last visit. It was then that Sister Faustina whispered to the priest the date of her death.

The dying sister also talked about a dreadful war that would come soon. Few paid attention to her, but she insisted just the same. "The war will be terrible and long," she stressed. To elderly Sister Anna, Sister Faustina said clearly, "A terrible war is coming, but our sisters will not have to leave this convent."

September passed into October. Mother Irene looked forward to her visits with the dying Sister Faustina There was always an atmosphere of tranquility around her.

"You'll see," Faustina said one day, "I will bring joy to our congregation." Mother's eyes opened wide, but she could see the simple faith in Faustina's face. She wasn't being proud. She was just telling the truth.

Shortly before her death, she whispered in Mother Irene's ear, "Jesus wants to make me a saint." Mother Irene looked into the face of the sister and could see Faustina's sincerity. She smiled and was silent.

"Jesus will come to take me home today," Faustina said softly to Sister Felicia, the sister on duty. It was October 5, 1938. Before the evening service at 7:00 PM, the community gathered around her bed and offered prayers. Faustina tried to form the words to join them. The sisters left the room quietly and went to bed. Only the sister on nursing duty was there at 10:45 PM, when Faustina took a turn for the worse.

The sister ran to get Sister Amelia Socha, but in her haste, she first knocked on the wrong door, accidentally rousing Sister Eufemia Traczynska. The young Sister Eufemia, understanding that Faustina must be near the end of her life, also hurried to the infirmary. Just after the sisters arrived at the bedside, Jesus called Sister Faustina home. She left this earth smiling peacefully. There would be no more worry, no more suffering, no more hurts—only eternal happiness in God's love. Sister Faustina was

"Jesus wants to make me a saint."

buried in the convent cemetery on October 7, 1938, the feast of the Holy Rosary.

The war that Sister Faustina predicted began a year after her death. It was indeed long and terrible. The Second World War lasted from 1939 until 1945. Poland was overrun by foreign invaders. Warsaw suffered terribly. True to Faustina's prophecy, the sisters in the convent where she died were able to remain there in safety for the entire war. Three times the Nazis threatened to send them away. Each time, the sisters ran to Sister Faustina's grave and begged for her protection. Each time, they were allowed to remain.

During the war, the devotion to Divine Mercy spread. Sister Faustina became known as the apostle of Jesus' mercy. Eventually, her diary, *Divine Mercy in My Soul*, was printed and translated. Prayer cards, images of the merciful Jesus, and the Chaplet of Divine Mercy made their way into churches and concentration camps throughout Poland. The war finally ended. Shrines honoring the merciful Jesus were built.

Then, because of some language difficulties and confusions, the devotion to Divine Mercy could not be promoted for nearly twenty years. With the misunderstandings finally overcome, the Church began to move ahead. In 1965, Archbishop Karol Wojtyla of Kraków, who had always had a deep interest in Sister Faustina and her message, re-opened an investigation into her life and her writings.

Would Sister Faustina be named blessed and eventually a saint? Witnesses were called to testify: her family, her neighbors, several sisters of her congregation, and many of those touched in some special way by the devotion to Divine Mercy. In 1968, the formal process for Faustina's beatification was begun.

On April 15, 1978, the ban against the devotion to Divine Mercy was lifted, mainly through the untiring efforts of the archbishop who had now become Cardinal Wojtyla. This proved to be quite a year for the devotion to Divine Mercy as well as for Cardinal Wojtyla. Six months later, Cardinal Wojtyla became Pope John Paul II!

One of this Pope's first official letters to the Church, on the infinite mercy of God, was called "Rich in Mercy." On April 18, 1993, Pope John Paul II declared Sister Faustina blessed. On April 30, 2000, she was canonized when the same Pope pronounced her a saint. On that great occasion, the Vatican officially established the Sunday after Easter as Divine Mercy Sunday throughout the world.

Jesus once told Sister Faustina, "I am sending you with my mercy to all humanity." Today, millions of people all over the globe continue to draw closer to God because of the humble life and writings of Saint Maria Faustina Kowalska, Jesus' messenger of mercy.

PRAYER

Saint Faustina, you have so much to teach us with your life. Jesus chose you to remind us that our Savior loves and accepts us as we are even as he calls us to greater holiness. You used all your energy to carry out God's plan for you. Your day-to-day life wasn't always easy. You were poor, and at times misunderstood by those who failed to recognize the love of Jesus in your heart. Jesus called the kingdom of heaven a treasure and a pearl of great price. You found that kingdom and that pearl in the Lord himself.

You preached Jesus' mercy with your life, with the Diary you wrote, and with the painting you had made. You never imagined all the good that Jesus would do through you. Saint Faustina, please teach me to love and trust in our most merciful Jesus. Amen.

THE DEVOTION TO
DIVINE MERCY

Jesus told Sister Faustina, "I am sending you with my message of mercy to all people. Speak about my mercy so everyone will know." Jesus promised Sister Faustina that, just as a loving mother cares for her baby, he will always take care of those who spread the honor of Divine Mercy.

Jesus' Divine Mercy means that he loves us even though we have sinned. The most important elements of the devotion to Divine Mercy are trust in our all-loving God and living in the spirit of merciful love toward our neighbors. Without trust in God and being loving and merciful toward our brothers and sisters, there can be no devotion to Divine Mercy.

God gave us, through Sister Faustina, four ways of practicing devotion to Divine Mercy:

1. The Image of the Merciful Jesus— Artists have created many versions of the image, but they all show the merciful Jesus. The red ray flowing from the area of his heart stands for blood, which is the life of the soul. The pale ray stands for the water of grace, which makes souls pure. We venerate (honor) the image, particularly on the Feast of Divine Mercy.

2. The Feast of Divine Mercy—The Sunday after Easter Sunday is Divine Mercy Sunday. To prepare for it, we should open and cleanse our hearts so that we may be ready to welcome Jesus. We do this by receiving the sacrament of Penance within several days before the Feast. We can also recite the Chaplet of Divine Mercy, which you will find on page 111, each day for nine days beginning on Good Friday. (Saying a particular prayer every day for nine days is called a *novena*.) Performing acts of kindness and mercy is an important preparation, and so is remembering to trust in God's mercy. On the Feast of Divine Mercy, we should receive Jesus in the Holy Eucharist, and we should be thankful for his goodness, and truly sorry for having hurt him by our sins. For those who fulfill these acts, Jesus promised complete forgiveness of sins and of punishment.

3. The Hour of Great Mercy—Jesus asked that every afternoon at 3:00 we remember his death on the cross and say a special prayer. We can pray quietly in our hearts, thinking of Jesus who was thinking of us and loving us on the cross. We can tell Jesus how much we love him and thank him for his goodness. We can say, "Oh Blood and Water, which gushed forth from the Heart of Jesus as a fount of mercy for us, I trust in You" (*Diary*, 84), or "Jesus, for the sake of your sorrowful passion, have mercy on us and on the whole world," or just simply, "Jesus, mercy."

4. The Chaplet of Divine Mercy—Here is the prayer that Jesus gave to Sister Faustina.

The Divine Mercy Chaplet is prayed on ordinary rosary beads as follows:

On the three beads near the crucifix, an Our Father, Hail Mary, and Apostles' Creed are said.

On the large bead before each decade:

Eternal Father, I offer You the Body and Blood, Soul and Divinity of Your dearly beloved Son, our Lord Jesus Christ, in atonement for our sins and those of the whole world.

On the ten small beads of each decade:

> For the sake of His sorrowful passion, have mercy on us and on the whole world.

When the five decades are completed, this prayer is said three times to conclude:

> Holy God, Holy Mighty One, Holy Immortal One, have mercy on us and on the whole world. (*Diary*, 476)

GLOSSARY

1. Anointing of the Sick—the sacrament in which the Holy Spirit strengthens and gives courage and peace to someone who is seriously ill. God's Spirit, through this sacrament, forgives sin and heals the soul.

2. Beatification—the ceremony in which the Catholic Church recognizes that a deceased person lived a life of gospel holiness in a heroic way. In most cases, a proven miracle obtained through the holy person's prayers to God is also required. A person who is beatified is given the title Blessed.

3. Canonization—the ceremony in which the pope officially declares that someone is a saint in heaven. To canonize someone is to recognize that he or she has lived a life of heroic virtue, is worthy of imitation, and can intercede for others. Like **beatification,** which it follows, canonization requires a miracle resulting from the holy person's prayers to God.

4. Cloistered order—a religious community that is dedicated to a hidden life of prayer. In cloistered communities, there are restrictions to the free entry of outsiders within certain areas. The most important work in these communities is prayer.

5. Conversion—a turning from a state of sin to repentance or from non-belief to faith.

6. Dormitory—a large room, or an entire building, in which many people sleep.

7. Dowry—an amount of money brought to a community by a woman religious upon entry.

8. Famine—extreme and general scarcity of food, as in a country or a large geographical area.

9. Novice—a person in the second period of training, the **novitiate,** that comes after postulancy and before the making of vows in religious life.

10. Novitiate—a period of time, now usually one or two years, in which **novices** who have responded to God's call to religious life grow in love for Jesus and in their desire to give themselves fully to him in the Church. Through prayer, study, and participation in their institute's life and mission, the novices learn about the spirit of the institute. They prepare to make the vows through which they will totally offer their lives to Jesus.

11. Penance—a prayer, sacrifice, or other action by which a person expresses sorrow for his or her sins.

12. Postulant—a person in the first stage of commitment to religious life, postulancy. Postulants ask to be admitted to the community as they learn what religious life will involve. The second stage in religious life is the **novitiate.**

13. Profession—the act of embracing the religious state by the three **religious vows** of poverty, chastity, and obedience. Today, for simple profession (first vows), a year or more of **novitiate** is necessary. After three or more years of simple profession, final profession may take place.

14. Purgatory—a place in which the souls of the just are purified after death and before they can enter heaven. It's important to pray for the souls in purgatory so they can go to heaven sooner.

15. Religious vow—an important promise made freely to God. The most common vows today are those of poverty, chastity, and obedience made by members of religious communities.

16. Rule (of religious life) — Organized methods of living in religious communities, prescribed by one in authority.

17. Smelling salts — a preparation of ammonia water, the smell of which was used to revive someone who was fainting.

18. Triduum — a period of three days of prayer, which may come before a special feast or may prepare for an important enterprise.

19. Tuberculosis — a disease that affects the lungs and may affect other parts of the body as well. Today tuberculosis is treatable and curable.

20. Veneration — paying honor with a ritual act of devotion to something or someone holy.

21. Vocation — a call from God to a certain lifestyle. A person may have a vocation to the married life, the priesthood, the religious life, or the single life. Everyone has a vocation to be holy.

Who are the
Daughters of St. Paul?

We are Catholic sisters with a mission. Our task is to bring the love of Jesus to everyone like Saint Paul did. You can find us in over 50 countries. Our founder, Blessed James Alberione, showed us how to reach out to the world through the media. That's why we publish books, make movies and apps, record music, broadcast on radio, perform concerts, help people at our bookstores, visit parishes, host JClub book fairs, use social media and the Internet, and pray for all of you.

Visit our Web site at www.pauline.org

BOOKS & MEDIA

The Daughters of St. Paul operate book and media centers at the following addresses. Visit, call, or write the one nearest you today, or find us at www.paulinestore.org.

CALIFORNIA
3908 Sepulveda Blvd, Culver City, CA 90230   310-397-8676
3250 Middlefield Road, Menlo Park, CA 94025   650-562-7060

FLORIDA
145 S.W. 107th Avenue, Miami, FL 33174   305-559-6715

HAWAII
1143 Bishop Street, Honolulu, HI 96813   808-521-2731

ILLINOIS
172 North Michigan Avenue, Chicago, IL 60601   312-346-4228

LOUISIANA
4403 Veterans Memorial Blvd, Metairie, LA 70006   504-887-7631

MASSACHUSETTS
885 Providence Hwy, Dedham, MA 02026   781-326-5385

MISSOURI
9804 Watson Road, St. Louis, MO 63126   314-965-3512

NEW YORK
115 E. 29th Street, New York City, NY 10016   212-754-1110

SOUTH CAROLINA
243 King Street, Charleston, SC 29401   843-577-0175

TEXAS
No book center; for parish exhibits or outreach evangelization, contact: 210-569-0500, or SanAntonio@paulinemedia.com, or P.O. Box 761416, San Antonio, TX 78245

VIRGINIA
1025 King Street, Alexandria, VA 22314   703-549-3806

CANADA
3022 Dufferin Street, Toronto, ON M6B 3T5   416-781-9131

¡También somos su fuente para libros, videos y música en español!